Social Responsibility as Academic Learning Course at the University

Ayseli Usluata

Social Responsibility as Academic Learning Course at the University

Bibliographic Information published by the Deutsche Nationalbibliothek
The Deutsche Nationalbibliothek lists this publication in the Deutsche Nationalbibliografie; detailed bibliographic data is available online at http://dnb.d-nb.de.

Library of Congress Cataloging-in-Publication Data
A CIP catalog record for this book has been applied for at the Library of Congress.

ISBN 978-3-631-85234-7 (Print)
E-ISBN 978-3-631-85434-1 (E-PDF)
E-ISBN 978-3-631-85435-8 (EPUB)
E-ISBN 978-3-631-85436-5 (MOBI)
DOI 10.3726/b18404

© Peter Lang GmbH
Internationaler Verlag der Wissenschaften
Berlin 2021
All rights reserved.

Peter Lang – Berlin · Bern · Bruxelles · New York · Istanbul · Oxford · Warszawa · Wien

All parts of this publication are protected by copyright. Any utilisation outside the strict limits of the copyright law, without the permission of the publisher, is forbidden and liable to prosecution. This applies in particular to reproductions, translations, microfilming, and storage and processing in electronic retrieval systems.

This publication has been peer reviewed.

www.peterlang.com

Contents

Introduction 7
    Social Responsibility Courses at a University: Academic
    Learning for Local and Global Solidarity 7

**Social Responsibility of Universities: Educating Young
People to Survive in a Globalizing World** 9
    New Century Began with a Consensus that Social
    Responsibility Education Needs to be Integrated into Higher
    Learning 12
    The Need for a New Kind of Education 12
    New Campus, New Community, New Courses 13
        Coexistence in the Globalising World 14
        Connecting the Young People of Different Nations 15
        An Innovative Way to Internationalise Learning in a
        Traditional Classroom 16
            "Global Classroom" 16
    Social Responsibility Project for Graduation and Local
    Community 17

**Social Responsibility Courses as Local and Global
Academic Learning** 27
    Global Classroom 28
    Reaction Papers about Stereotyping 34
    "Social Responsibility Course" 36
    "Here We Are" A Call to the Women of Kayışdağı for Solidarity .. 37
    "Social Responsibility Project for Graduation" Course 41

Contents

- At the Care Home in Kayışdağı 41
  - A Handful of Love and Respect 42
  - Loneliness in a Crowd 42
  - Concluding Comments by Students 43
- Breaking Down the Walls 50
  - Change a Child, the Whole World Changes! 50
  - Great Love of Tiny Hearts 50
  - Love Increases When Shared 50
  - A Chance to Change Local and Global Communities with Children 51
  - Achievements 52
  - What Our Senior Students as Teachers Learned 52
  - Reactions 53
  - Children to Change the Society/Nation 57
- Hello Life! 59
  - Young students who need special attention 59
  - Reflection 60
- Joint Intergenerational Activities 64
- Social Responsibility Projects During the Lockdown 2020 70
  - A Collection from the Project Stories and Comments of Students 71
- What the Students' Reflection Papers Reveal 89

Introduction

Social Responsibility Courses at a University: Academic Learning for Local and Global Solidarity

Two undergraduate courses, "Social Responsibility Project for Graduation" and "Global (Intercultural Communication) Classroom", were included in the syllabus of the Public Relations and Publicity Department of Yeditepe University, Istanbul, Turkey, in the beginning of the 21st century to prepare young university students for social and global awareness.

The future of all societies depends upon young people who need to experience activities that are challenging, inspiring, and educative. Social responsibility education programmes, through courses, educate young people on how to become active participants in the process of making positive social changes. Literature review reveals the importance of including social responsibility courses in the curricula of universities to provide young students with guidance and a sense of purpose.

After working at the two best and well-known public universities of Turkey, a new position with the responsibility of founding a new department was a challenge for an academician. A new private university with liberal education principles could respond by offering service-learning courses, relating projects to the world outside academia or connecting students to the students of universities in foreign countries. The new academic learning courses in the academic curriculum, with the responsibility to educate young people who will add new values to society, would foster the development of the behaviour and social responsibility of the privileged students and show that they can respond to actual social issues.

The green campus of the new university was surrounded by walls, and what we can do for the local community outside the walls was the question of our "Social Responsibility Project for Graduation" course. One group of students in the course wanted to reach the women inhabitants, declaring, "We are here for you!" Another group of students, inviting the primary school children to the campus, said, "We are overthrowing the walls and opening the gates to be your teachers." The group who chose to visit the care home in the neighbourhood added a new name, "From 7 to

77," making the project intergenerational. Student enthusiasm influencing the quality of life in the local community, Kayışdağı, created solidarity for successful coexistence.

The language of instruction at Yeditepe University is English, so knowing a second language is a privilege, delegating the students the responsibility of connecting with the university students in foreign countries, exchanging ideas and promoting their cultures. Our "Intercultural Communication" course, joining the Global Classroom Project of UNL (University of Nebraska-Lincoln) each semester through video conferencing, allows students to talk face-to-face and transfer knowledge. Skills gained in the classroom are put into practice, and students become global citizens who are more socially aware and active.

A course may be contributing to the local community or an international or global one, both are important activities that help students retain and improve their skills, providing opportunities to explore new options. One of the aims of academic learning was through guided but independent efforts to develop intercultural behaviour globally and locally. Narrative reflections and pictures, as well as comments of the students and the local people which have been collected for fifteen years, will be shared and discussed.

Sustainability/ Further Developments – These academic learning courses can be inspiring to other universities. Social responsibility of universities should not be an extra-curricular activity; universities should answer to the needs of their own communities and the needs of the globalizing world offering academic learning courses. We have discovered that students full of energy can be prospective change makers.

It should be noted that this Project received coverage in both local and national magazines and newspapers and EMIL award.

Social Responsibility of Universities: Educating Young People to Survive in a Globalizing World

> What is needed is opening minds
> to the complexity of the world and of human thought
> and opening hearts to the diversity of human
> experience and feeling.
>
> Martin J Gannon

Since the start of the century, the proposal for a new position with the responsibility of founding a new department at a new university inspired me to rethink what is expected from universities in this century of change. Considering the crucial role universities play in young people's lives, their social responsibility can be questioned. "Social responsibility theory" articulates their obligation to serve the public, and education has the potential to help young university students acquire the necessary knowledge, skills, values and motivation to take action as thoughtful, caring and responsible citizens within communities. Berkowitz (1997) points out that education inevitably affects character, either intentionally or unintentionally, and being socially responsible means that people and organisations must behave ethically and with sensitivity and question whether their actions will improve the lives of others.

Research results published in the magazines of institutions of higher education reveal, and academics agree, that universities are faced with the need to change their established structures and curricula to keep up with the changing times by strengthening social role of education and promoting shared and universal human values. Universities' commitment to social responsibility and the learning outcomes necessary for all university students to become global citizens in the twenty-first century have been the research topics of academics and educational institutions all over the world. The results of their studies have expressed the need of universities to provide an education that meets the challenges of the globalising world and the need of young people to be agents of social development as responsible citizens. In responding to new challenges, some universities have already made social responsibility their guiding principle.

In his article "Only Connect", William Cronon (1998) declares that universities, while strengthening their civic role, can also promote shared and universal human values. "Universities should provide students with a sense of social and civic responsibility—they as advocates of their thoughtful judgements—can make a difference" (1999) wrote Eugene M. Lang, an educational philanthropist who in 1963 founded an organisation called Project Pericles. The 2002 national report by the Association of American Colleges and Universities (AAC&U) provided a descriptive picture of how educating "responsible" learners can have an influence beyond the college campus: "The future of any society depends upon the character and competence of its young, and in order to develop character and competence, young people need guidance to provide them with direction and a sense of purpose". The theme of the summer/fall 2005 issue of the *Association of American Colleges and Universities* magazine was "Educating for Personal and Social Responsibility", requesting "A Review of the Literature" (AAC&U 2005). In their article, Richard H. Hersh and Carol Geary Schneider emphasised the need for higher education to do more for the development of personal and social responsibility (AAC&U 2005). In the winter 2009 issue of *Liberal Education*, Anne Colby and William M. Sullivan identify five key dimensions of personal and social responsibility as (a) striving for excellence, (b) cultivating personal and academic integrity, (c) contributing to a larger community, (d) taking seriously the perspectives of others and (e) developing competence in ethical and moral reasoning (*Liberal Education* 2009).

In 2010, Jan R. Liss and Ariane Liazos discussed the necessity of "Incorporating Education and Social Responsibility into the Undergraduate Curriculum" in *Change: The Magazine of Higher Learning* (Liss & Liazos 2010, pp. 45–50). They argue that student interest in civic engagement has resulted in increased opportunities to volunteer on campuses; without the support of the academic curricula, however, these benefits are short-lived: "To educate students for socially responsible and participatory citizenship, colleges and universities need to expand their curricula, adopt new courses, and revise old ones" was their suggestion.

Identifying the need for global citizenship in an increasingly interconnected world, Nel Noddings draws attention to the need to empower young people with transferable skills and civic engagement in "Educating students for Global Awareness" (Noddings 2005). According to the United Nations, Global Citizenship Education (GCED) provides skills and values students' needs to resolve the interconnected challenges of the 21st century. UNESCO has developed curricula guidance planning education for improved outcomes in these areas.

Referencing Albert Einstein's famous statement, "We can't solve problems by using the same kind of thinking we used when we created them", the University of Graz in Austria established a new course to respond to the present day's challenges. UNESCO and "Teaching and Learning for a Sustainable Future: A Multimedia Teacher Programme" of the Global University Network for Innovation (GUNİ) supported the GUNİ Graz–Stria conference held to discuss the social responsibility of the universities (2007). On March 22, 2007 "Social Responsibility of Higher Education Institutions" was the theme of a conference held in Tel-Aviv.

The Universidad Construye Pais Project (2006) began working on the concept of social responsibility in 2002. The working definition of social responsibility in Latin America within this project was "participative dialogue with society to promote sustainable human development" (Vallaeys, 2007). Students were expected to answer to their own communities in both the present and future, as well as to globalised society; in addition, universities would answer the needs of Latin America and the world. As a "productive dialogue", educating for personal and social responsibility would be the contribution of higher education to students' moral and ethical development. Furthermore, according to this project, universities' primary aim should not be to prepare workers for the global market because what the global world needs is young people who recognise the discrepancy between what is and what could or should be.

New Century Began with a Consensus that Social Responsibility Education Needs to be Integrated into Higher Learning

While all these studies, conferences and articles concerned about how to educate young people for the new century were taking place, in Turkey we must find an answer to how to educate our university students to become socially responsible citizens of Turkey as well as the global world. Young "modern" people in Turkey are generally stereotyped as self-centred and uninterested in social problems. This may be because of Turkey's individualistic education system, nuclear families and a hectic city lifestyle which isolates people and makes them more egocentric. For the future of the country, in order to become global citizens and agents of social development, an increasing number of young people need social responsibility education. Since education has the potential to help young university students acquire the necessary knowledge, skills, values and motivation to take action in their communities, they can make a difference as thoughtful, engaged and socially responsible citizens. For the future of a culture that used to be collectivist and where family solidarity was once valued, young people educated with social responsibility can decide which elements to keep and which to change.

The inclusion of a social responsibility courses in the curriculum can educate young people not only for social needs but also to add new values to society. According to Paolo Freire, it is the educator's ability to empower young people for social transformation that is realised by critical engagement with one's community and the world. These words have the power to motivate educators.

The Need for a New Kind of Education

> *"Education is an Act of Love and Thus an Act of Courage"*
>
> –Paulo Freire

In the beginning of the twenty-first century, after working at two precious universities, Middle East Technical University in Ankara and Boğaziçi University in İstanbul, and having gained invaluable experiences, I was ready to prepare for a new academic life as the head of a new department within the communication faculty of Yeditepe University, a private university founded by Bedrettin Dalan, the former mayor of Istanbul, in 1996, and which had moved to a new campus in 2000. The university's aim was "to raise young people that are modern, inquisitive, well-versed in different cultures and personally well developed". These principles could motivate an educator to act with courage, allowing her to incorporate new courses into the undergraduate curriculum with the responsibility to educate young people who, as well as adding new values to the society, will be the young people the global world needs. In April 1992 as the director of the "International Studies Center" arranging a "Peace Studies Conference" we had discussed the possibility of incorporating "Peace Education" in the curriculums of universities with the academics invited from different countries. With its contemporary academic programs and applications, Yeditepe University could be ready to offer an education that is necessary for people of the changing age. Thus, all that was needed was "an act of courage", according to Freire.

New Campus, New Community, New Courses

The campus of the university is located in Kayışdağı, a district in the hills of the Asian side of Istanbul. As a city, İstanbul was founded on seven hills, as alluded to in the name of the university, Yeditepe (seven-hill). Kayışdağı is a district of Istanbul province, which is named after the third of the city's seven hills. The green campus is surrounded by high walls with two gates near both a forest and the district of Kayışdağı, a lower-middle income area. A new community can be discovered outside the walls of the beautiful campus by the new, privileged students of a private university.

Believing that universities play a crucial role in young people's lives, it would be exciting to try to find an answer to the questions of what the students can do for the neighbours and what they can learn from their active participation in questioning and trying to find solutions. Since education affects character, being exposed to social problems in and around campus can help young students acquire the ability to solve problems (Youniss & Yates 1997). That is why higher education institutions in the past two decades have started to make social responsibility one of their guiding principles, taking an approach to learning that helps students develop a sense of responsibility.

Individual social responsibility includes each person's engagement towards the community where he or she lives, which can take the form of interest in what is happening in the community, as well as active participation in solving local problems. As the young people of the globalising world, however, students also have the responsibility to become members of the global world. As an instructor of "Intercultural Communication", my course objective, in addition to gaining intercultural competence, includes social responsibility and the ability to engage effectively in regional, national and global communities. William Cronon's article "Only Connect" (1998), referencing a statement from E.M. Forster, was the motivation for me to go forward and remembering the words of Freire for the educators I was ready to realize my dream and connect young students with both local and global communities.

Educational programs connecting the universities with the local and global communities through their offered courses can allow students to use their knowledge and skills to the benefit of the communities in which they live, as well as global communities with the knowledge of their civic responsibility. Courses connecting students to the local community or an international community can help students retain and improve their intercultural communication skills, provide opportunities to explore new options and become active participants in the process of making positive social changes.

Coexistence in the Globalising World

Two undergraduate courses, "Social Responsibility Project for Graduation" and "Global Classroom", were proposed to be included in the undergraduate course schedule of the Public Relations and Publicity Department of the Faculty of Communication at Yeditepe University, my new university, with the aim of promoting social awareness and motivating young university students to contribute to local, national and global communities. Exchanging ideas would raise awareness and students would learn how to behave empathetically towards both the local people and the young university students from a different country, "only through connecting".

Connecting the Young People of Different Nations

International conferences are the best occasions for academicians to exchange ideas and get feedback. At the 1999 conference in Finland at the University of Jyvaskyla (1999), "Living and Learning Together in the 21st Century", I presented a paper, "Communication Education: Need for Critical Approach towards Mass Media and Awareness of Cultural Differences". When I complained about the news media treating my country as producing only bad news, a colleague told me that he no longer got the news from traditional news media but from the internet. That inspired me as well as my colleagues who were thinking about finding a way to connect through the internet via e-mail. At Boğaziçi University, where I was teaching business communication, the language of instruction was English. Knowing a second language was a privilege for the students, who could connect with the students of universities in other countries, but my personal desire for these young people was for them to assume the responsibility of promoting their culture and country. Connecting with the students at universities of other countries, they could exchange ideas about their cultures. At Boğaziçi University, at the initiation of colleagues teaching intercultural and business communication at universities in Germany, Denmark and Canada, we started an e-mail exchange program. The results were exciting and beneficial for the students of both partner universities. I continued the same project with the students taking the "İntercultural Communication" course at Yeditepe University, since the university's language of instruction is English.

We shared the results of our individual e-mail exchange projects at the international conferences with the conference participants. We presented the paper we prepared with Professor Carol Sevitt from Ryerson University, Toronto, Canada on "E-Mail Exchanges Between Students in Toronto and Istanbul Lead to Intercultural Understanding" at the ABC Conference, Cincinnati, Ohio (2002) and I presented my paper on "Communicating across the borders: A project to find out who the others are: Intercultural Competencies in a Globalized World" at the SIETAR Vienna Congress, Austria (2002).

An Innovative Way to Internationalise Learning in a Traditional Classroom

"Global Classroom"

In May 2004 I was among a group of academicians Yeditepe University sent to the United States to visit universities there. At the University of Nebraska–Lincoln, I mentioned this personal project in my communication courses and showed the department magazine (PRP) that our students were publishing each semester and the interesting evaluation of the students published in the magazine. To my surprise, we learned that UNL was part of the "Global Classroom" project, and Dr Charles Braithwaite was the instructor in charge of the project.

According to Dr Braithwaite, "Global classrooms" represent one form of virtual, collaborative education where students in different parts of the world can share joint learning experiences in real time. In essence, global classrooms involve developing a curriculum in which instructors and students find an innovative way to internationalise learning in a traditional classroom and teach and learn with their peers abroad, using Internet-based technologies for communication.

We wanted to be part of the project, and Dr Braithwaite, along with the technical director, visited our university. The following semester, we saw him and his students on the screen of the video conference. A new course, "Global Communication", became an undergraduate course in the syllabus and revealed both the common and different sides of the two countries and cultures. For 15 years, we have been connecting each semester, and the students have become the young people of the global world.

Internationalising education offered important learning outcomes. Dr Braithwaite said, "I'd like our students to truly understand that they are members of a global society and [explore] how technology can be used to learn and share ideas around the world". "Most of the time students just hear 30-second sound bites on CNN about what's happening around the world; now they get to talk with students who are there about political issues", said Dr Braithwaite who helped launch the Global Classroom course in 2005

In the globalising world, intercultural communication allows students to transfer the knowledge and skills gained in the classroom to practical projects. In the "Global Classroom", face-to-face communication with American university students facilitated better communication and allowed the students to communicate in English, exchange stories about their families and hometowns, share ideas, ask questions and learned about each other's daily lives. The course gave the student a better understanding of different beliefs and lifestyles and helped them build cross-national bridges.

Meaningful integration among students from two different countries helped our students grow as individuals by sharing their ideas, stories, daily lives, behaviour and customs; this opened a new door to them, and they became more socially and internationally aware and active.

Social Responsibility Project for Graduation and Local Community

Forster's idea to "only connect" could work for the local community as well; after connecting with our neighbours, however, we also need to remember the words of J. Bronowski, a humanist intellectual who emphasised the importance of understanding and closing the distance between individuals: "We have to touch people" (Bronowski 1973). We tried to find an answer to our question "How can our students connect?" and "touch" the local community around the campus in the neighbouring community of the district of Kayışdağı. Middle or low-income families live in Kayışdağı: 50 % of the inhabitants are women and 62 % are elementary or high-school graduates. We had to find answers to a lot of questions: for example, what do the neighbours think about the privileged young students studying at a private university, driving their cars through the local community, parking their cars along the walls that separate the campus from the local community and entering the campus through the grand elevated gates? Are the students at the university aware of the problems in the neighbouring community? In a globalised society that values consumption, what kind of young people are we educating? What are the students' consumption values? What are the obligations of the privileged young students to the community or society in which they live? Our last questions were "What can we do for them?" and "What can our students learn from them?" Here we must remember Cronon's expectations of the educated young people embodying values such as "to listen and to hear", "to be able to talk with anyone", and "to practice humility, tolerance and self-criticism".

With its contemporary academic programs, Yeditepe University was the right university to offer a student-centred course which is necessary for personally well-developed, thoughtful students who are aware of their responsibility to the community and society in which they live. Through this course, we could educate young people to become active participants in community development and produce positive social changes in the quality of life in communities. Young people are generally stereotyped as self-interested or uninterested in social problems. A social responsibility course would allow the students to be involved in solving the problems of the local people and help them become more thoughtful and responsible individuals and using their knowledge and skills will make them aware of their role in society. Such educational programs connect the universities with the local community.

Fostering and developing the mindsets of students affect both their personal development and the social development of their community. Their behaviour while communicating shows how skilful they are; with empathy, students can learn how to behave towards the local people.

I am thankful to Yeditepe University for its foundational principles that allowed us to incorporate social responsibility as a new course in the undergraduate syllabus of the department. Incorporating such a service-oriented course meant taking initiative on behalf of universities in Turkey.

In this course, the roles and responsibilities of the individual in society and what we can do for our neighbours, the local community, are questioned. While trying to find answers to these questions, students' opinions were very helpful. The aim of the course was to build a culture of solidarity comprising individuals who are responsible and supportive. Once started, the project was completely under the control of the students, who were provided only with guidance.

After a field study questioning what we could do for our neighbours, the first reaction came from a group of students who wanted to announce: "Here We are!" to neighbouring women. Their aim was to determine the needs of the homemakers living in the vicinity of the university campus and help them.

The next group wanted to open the doors of the campus to invite primary-school children to the campus, declaring "We are Breaking Down the Wall". The parents had concerns for their daughters and sons being unable to get a satisfactory education.

After learning about a care home for the elderly in the neighbourhood, a group of students wanted to visit them. Recently, a workshop school for disabled young people needed help from us, and our students were excited to become their social friends.

The project continued in groups every semester according to the proposals of the students, which were:

1. education-related (serving as teachers and role models for primary-school children),
2. philanthropic (visiting the elderly in the care homes for moral support) and recently
3. empathic and unifying (visiting the work-school for disabled young people that started in 2017).

Weekly schedules for the school children were planned in a week in either the morning or the afternoon, according to the school schedule. The primary-school children were brought by their parents to the main gate of the university, where they were met by our students, who took them to a classroom in our building via shuttle bus. Acting as big sisters and big brothers, our students became their teachers of English, maths, social science, children's rights, the internet and sport. They all played basketball and volleyball on the university courts, watched movies, got help with their homework and, most importantly, learned from their "role models" about the proper behaviour and manners needed to help the children grow as responsible adults.

Weekly schedules for the elderly were planned for particular days in a week, when our students, either individually or in small groups of two or three, participated in daily visits to the elderly care home. During these visits, students talked to the residents, asked them what they needed, listened to their personal histories, looked at their old photos and helped them read their letters or magazines. Additionally, they helped the residents make telephone calls, sang songs together and brought them small presents and homemade food that they might miss.

Joint activities were organised by the students to bring two generations together (becoming three or four generations altogether) at the university, where they attended concerts and dance performances, sang songs, watched movies, and had dinner. Additional activities have included a boat trip along the Bosporus, a picnic, a visit to a toy museum (for which the university provided transportation) and other social events.

For twelve years, senior students from the PRP Department have been actively participating in social-responsibility projects in groups. Every semester, students build a culture of solidarity between generations with the primary school children and the care home residents. This is the inspiration for our students' calling their project "From 7 to 77". Guided but independent efforts have been contributing positively to the local community, and the students in the communication faculty have practised Communication Accommodation Theory (CAT) in their relations with individuals from different generations.

In terms of the projects' significance and value, "student idealism" has been transformed into action and fostered a deeper sense of commitment among the students. Additionally, the project has met some needs in the local community regarding education and elder care.

Regarding the community, the project brought excitement to primary-school children, opened up new horizons for them, motivated them to set goals for their education and gave them "big sisters" and "big brothers" as role models. They children wrote letters and made pictures to express how much they loved their "student teachers". Additionally, their parents were consistently grateful and thankful. They all look forward to bringing their children back the following semester.

For the residents of the elder care home, the young university students were like daughters or sons: they wrote poems for them and the residents said they counted the hours while waiting for their visits. The elder residents received warm and sincere involvement, care and attention from the young people, who listened to their stories and shared their pictures with patience, who danced with them, sang songs with them and made them happy for a few hours to help them forget their loneliness.

The university students gained insights into: (1) the problems of old age and loneliness when they met with the elderly homeless, (2) how the traditional Turkish family structure after modernisation has sometimes excluded grandparents and (3) the need to provide educational and social support for young children when it is unavailable from home or in their overcrowded classes. As committed and engaged young people, the university students began to rethink their own stereotypes about the community outside the walls of the campus. Their comments after these experiences demonstrate that the project has the potential to help students acquire the values and motivation to be thoughtful and socially responsible individuals.

Regarding sustainability and further developments, this course can inspire other universities. It is clear that a one-semester experience is too short to accomplish all of our goals. Offering the course each semester, however, overcomes this limitation. Universities' social responsibility should not be an extra-curricular activity; rather, universities should answer the needs of their communities. We have discovered that students full of energy can be prospective change-makers, making a difference in people's lives. We know that the story of this course can be inspiring to other universities.

Students completed their "Social Responsibility for Graduation" course, calling it "From 7 to 77" Intergenerational Solidarity".

It should be noted that this project received coverage in both local and national magazines and newspapers, not to mention the thank-you letters from nine-year-old kids.

Turkish papers and magazines publishes the works of the students..

Concluding comments by students include:

"We built a 'Bridge Between Generations', established a connection with them every week and shared our feelings, thoughts and especially 'smiles' ".

"I now know that there is no happiness greater than making other people happy—just holding hands may be enough".

"Every day I went there with excitement and left with peace in my heart".

"Thank you for assigning us such a great responsibility".

"They all left unforgettable traces in our lives".

Thank you to BJF (Beth Johnson Foundation) for the permission to use our pictures and stories published in EMIL newsletter.

My special thanks to Julie Melville, who was the coordinator of EMIL (European Map of Intergenerational Learning) for motivating us to send the pictures and stories of our Project to the EMIL newsletter.

2013 EMIL Intergenerational Learning Awards Programme – Winners Announced

Through the Awards Programme, EMIL has been able to highlight and showcase existing examples throughout Europe where intergenerational work adds value. Through a nomination process, award winners have demonstrated innovative and sustainable projects working with people of all ages that have made a real impact.

The winners are:
Communities – "From 7 to 77" Solidarity between generations & Generations for Peace
Housing/Environment – Intergenerational Apartments
Culture & the Arts – mix@ges – Intergenerational Bonding via Creative New Media
Working Environment/Employment – Young and Old in School
Other – Have your Say

Our publication – **EMIL AWARDS PROGRAMME REPORT**: *A European Perspective on Examples of Intergenerational Learning & Practice* provides case studies from all shortlisted nominations from the Awards Programme. Thank you to everyone who participated in the Awards programme. We were certainly pleased with the amount & quality of nominations submitted. Congratulations again to the winners of this year's awards. We are already planning, and look forward to hosting the awards programme again next year.
EMIL@bjf.org.uk

"We are currently in the midst of planning our ECIL conference and wanted to reach out to you now to officially invite you to our conference. As part of the conference we have dedicated 1.5 hrs to showcase examples of best practice in the field of intergenerational learning throughout Europe. The three of you have submitted such examples during our EMIL Awards programme and we would very much like it if you could attend the conference – conduct a 15 min presentation and be available for questions and then take part in our conference for the day".

18 September 2014, Sophia, Bulgaria

As an EMIL Award recipient of last year for our social responsibility project "from 7 to 77" I was invited to present our project as an example of good practice at the conference.

"Learning to make society for all generations"—a final event of project ECIL—The Development of a Certificate in Intergenerational which took place in Sophia on Sept. 18, 2014.

Heartfelt thanks to the PRP graduates who all contributed to the project "Promoting Intergenerational Learning" during the last semester of their academic life. These were the first steps to create "a society for all generations".

References

Association of American Colleges and Universities (AAC&U). (2002). Greater Expectations: A New Vision for Learning as a Nation Goes to College, the national report.

Association of American Colleges and Universities (AAC&U). (2005). Requesting "A Review of the Literature" on "Educating for Personal and Social Responsibility." Summer/Fall Issue.

Berkowitz, M. W. (1997). The Complete Moral Person: Anatomy and Formation. In *Moral Issues in Psychology: Personalist Contributions to Selected Problems*, ed. J. M. Dubois, 11–41. Lanham, MD: University Press of America.

Bronowski, J. (1973). *Ascent of Man* [Television series], episode 1 aired 1 March 1975.

Colby, A., Sullivan, W. M. (2009). "Strengthening the Foundations of Students' Excellence, Integrity, and Social Contribution." *Liberal Education* 95(1), 22–29.

Cronon, W. (1998). "Only Connect (1998). The Goals of a Liberal Education." *American Scholar* 67(4, Autumn).

"Decoding the Signs: Communicating across the boarders: Intercultural Competencies in a Globalized World." (Oct. 22–26, 2002). ABC 67th Annual International Convention, Cincinnati, OH.

Eugene, M. (1999). Civic Engagement in the Classroom: Strategies for Educational Philanthropist Who in 1963 Founded an Organization Called Project Pericles.

Hersh, R., Schneider, C. G. (2005). "Fostering Personal and Social Responsibility on College and University Campuses." *Liberal Education* 91 (3, Summer/Fall).

"Intercultural Encounter: E-Mail Exchanges Between Students in Toronto and Istanbul Lead to Intercultural Understanding." (April 2002). SIETAR Europa, Vienna, Austria.

Liss, J. R., Liazos, A. (2010). "Incorporating Education for Civic and Social Responsibility into the Undergraduate Curriculum". Change: *The Magazine of Higher Learning* 42(1), 45–50.

Noddings, N. (2005). *Educating Citizens for Global Awareness*. Teachers' College Columbia University, New York/London.

Youniss, J., Yates, M. (1997). *Community Service and Social Responsibility in Youth*. The University of Chicago Press Books.

Social Responsibility Courses as Local and Global Academic Learning

Academic Learning Courses offering social responsibility may contribute to the local community or the whole country or an international or global community; all are important activities that help students retain and improve their skills and provide opportunities to explore new options,

Two courses have opened two doors for the young students: one to the campus for the local community and one between the young American and Turkish students.

Through video conferencing, the "Global Classroom" course connects our students with the American students at UNL, and the "Social Responsibility project" course connects the students with the local people near the campus, helping the young university students grow as individuals by providing them with insights to other cultures and customs. The two courses allow students to "Break Down the Walls" between the countries and between the local community and the students on campus.

Communication connects the students with people from different cultures and with different customs, giving them insights into different beliefs, lifestyles, cultures and customs that help students grow as individuals, becoming more socially and internationally aware and active.

Social integration is the creation of relationships and understanding across different social as well as national groups.

The courses are designed to empower students to become more thoughtful and effective citizens and build a culture of solidarity that is supportive.

A new private university with liberal education principles can respond to the need to offer academic learning courses and a course incorporating a social responsibility project into the undergraduate curriculum, as well as an intercultural communication course becoming part of the solution to social challenges that takes the responsibility to educate young people who will add new values to the society.

In this globalizing world, intercultural communication allows students to transfer the knowledge and skills they have gained in the classroom to practical projects in collaboration with the students of a university in a different country, thus a course fostering the development of the students' social responsibilities. This course encourages students to stop being passive observers of social phenomena and instead, through active participation, have a direct effect on solving current social issues. The course's "Contribution to the Community" project is an important activity that helps students retain and improve their skills, provides them with an opportunity to explore new options, gives them the pleasure of participating in solving community problems and contributes to building their problem-solving capacity.

Global Classroom

In order to survive in the interdependent global society without violating the norms and rules, we have to provide a broader education and help young people become caring, conscious and contributing world citizens. They can collaboratively build the future of human society.

Good morning! NEBRASKA-LINCOLN UNIVERSITY

Good afternoon! YEDİTEPE UNIVERSITY

Thank you

Teşekkürler

Partnership with the "Global Classroom Project" started in 2005, and since then every semester students, changing each semester, on Tuesdays Turkish students in the afternoon and American students in the morning, have been saying "Hello" to each other. They introduce themselves with power point slides and talk face-to-face.

Instructors of the course: Dr. Charles Braithwaite, in Nebraska-Lincoln University, and Prof. Dr. Ayseli Usluata in Yeditepe University.

Global classroom creates a healthy learning environment where students learn to accept and respect differences. In this class students also learn about themselves and their cultures.

The reflection paper of the exchange student from Germany Philip Borchert who took our "Global Communication" course: "Intercultural Communication students from Communication Studies 211 and their professor Dr. Charles Braithwaite, welcomed Turkish children to their video class with Yeditepe University in Istanbul with Dr. Ayseli Usluata. The Children made a **Hello Nebraska** sign, sang songs, and talked about Turkey's National Sovereignty and Children's Day, which takes place on April 23 each year."

30 Social Responsibility Courses as Local and Global Academic Learning

Prof. James Milliken, President of The University of Nebraska (2009) attended our "Global Classroom" and addressed the students of both universities: "I was invited because I made statements publicly about the importance of exchange programs. We are preparing our students for the coming century. In 10 minutes I learned something about Turkey that I didn't know before. In the US, we have Mothers' Day and Fathers' Day and I have three Children who ask me why we don't have Children's Day! Perhaps we should follow you and celebrate Children's Day in the US…"

Mr. Bedrettin Dalan, founder of Yeditepe University and said: "I am very happy to see your cooperation with our university and hope it will continue. This is a very good model! The young generation all over the world is the same, I see my sons and daughters as in here. I wish you all the best hoping you will come to our university--in the summer school, we have all the facilities and the dormitories… I wish you can make a stronger cooperation with Prof. Dr. Ayseli Usluata and hope you can visit us with your students. All the best"

Dr. Braithwaite kindly found and gave all his students "Turkish Evil eye beads" which are supposed to bring good luck for us Turks and American students are learning and enjoying a different custom or belief. Interaction with students of another culture provided students with opportunities to share ideas, experiences, and different perspectives. During their interactions while considering issues from personal, local, national and global perspectives students develop their own perspective. From their reactions show their perception of the other culture

The reflection paper of the exchange student from Germany Philip Borchert who took our "Global Communication" course:

When I first heard about the "global classroom" as part of the subject intercultural communication I was very excited and curious how it will be like. I am always very interested in meeting new people from different cultures and I thought that this would be a great opportunity for me to learn more about the American culture on the one hand but of course on the other hand about the Turkish culture. Therefore I considered the idea of having a videoconference with the students from Nebraska as a very interesting one.

When attending the first class I was stunned by the technological advancement that the sound and video quality was that good. That made it possible to have an as real as possible interaction in which body language and facial expressions could be seen, which is very important when learning more about another culture.

In the past 3 ½ years in which I have been living abroad I realised how important it is in intercultural communication to reflect about the self and to be aware about yourself and your personality to put aside your ethnocentrism. That is a good start to gain self-awareness and I think it is a good exercise to sometimes think about yourself and try to find out who you are. Hence we did not only learn about a different culture but also about ourselves. Though both cultures valued their families very much the Turkish culture is still much more family oriented than the American culture or the German culture.

Thanks to Dr. Chuck Braithwaite, favourite professor of his Turkish students.

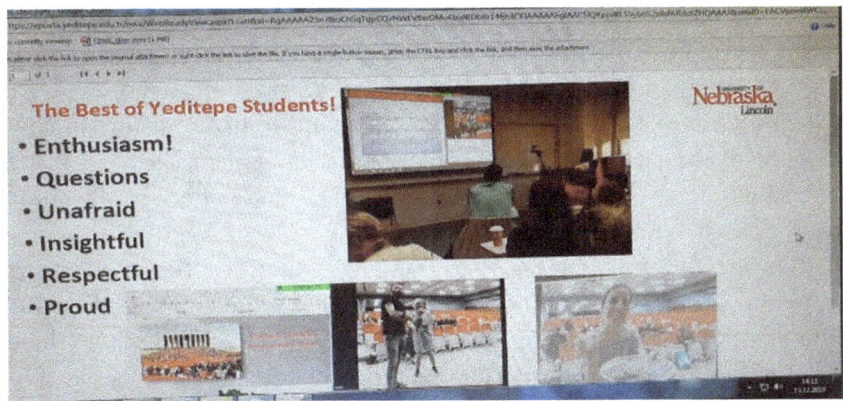

Reaction Papers about Stereotyping

"I do think there is some stereotyping that has occurred during our interaction with Turkey and the students there. In my mind I don't think I see it as stereotyping, yet it kind of is because I am forming opinions on Turkey and its people from a very small sample of the population."

"One of the first things I noticed about the Turkish students is that they seemed somewhat more open and friendly than my classmates and I. It seems as though they are not uncomfortable at all by waving at the camera and saying "Hi" with great energy and enthusiasm. As Americans, I feel like we are instilled with more of a timid, shy approach to people we are not familiar with. Now, this may go into the introvert – extrovert kind of thing. This has seemed to make us much more conversational during our session. I know I always think to myself, "Wow, class really flew by today" because we were so engrossed in what was being talked about with Turkey"."

"As a class we have also talked many times about how relationships are extremely important to Turkey's people. I would have to say I stereotype them as being more carefree and enjoyable with everyday life than the average American. We as Americans are raised in a cutthroat environment where one must work extremely hard to get ahead in order to have a "good life". We are so busy as individuals that we rarely take time out of our busy schedules just to go out with a friend, relax with relatives, or simply slow down. Honestly, it is something I really admire about them. There are many times I wish I was not nearly as busy and could kind of do what I wanted to from time to time."

"During our interactions with Turkey, I didn't notice any strong stereotypes; however I did notice that there were a few things that were different. An example might be the family discussion we had in class, where the Turkish students might presume our family doesn't matter as much to us as their families do to them."

"First of all, I have to say that the Americans are not exactly what I thought. They are very different in character, in lifestyle, in view of life, in behavior and in social life. It was very interesting to see how we came from different cultures, from sitting in class to speaking styles. At first we started to communicate with "Who am I" presentations. For the first time,

I had the opportunity to introduce myself to people from different cultures through video technology and answered the questions with pleasure".

"I felt what ''Global Citizen" means thanks to this course. I realized again that each person is valuable in this world after conversations that we had with the students from Nebraska. Everyone in the world has many things to learn from the people of other nationalities. I think that this course has improved my abilities in communication. I am sure that I will be able to use this knowledge and experience in all areas of my life." Cihan Eşen

"There are some ways we have stereotyped Turkish students too. For me personally before we started actually talking with the Turkish students I made the assumption that most of them would be Muslim because they are from a "Muslim" country. Little did I know that Turkey is actually quite religiously free unlike most other Muslim cultures."

"Both students got along well with each other. Both students has hobbies and dreams. Turkish and American students were aware of global developments. Both students had after graduate foals."

36 Social Responsibility Courses as Local and Global Academic Learning

"Social Responsibility Course"

The green Campus of Yeditepe University at Kayışdağı on the Asian side of Istanbul.

The local community of Kayışdağı live in the neighborhood around the campus.

"Here We Are" A Call to the Women of Kayışdağı for Solidarity

"Individual social responsibility includes the engagement of each person in the community where he or she lives, which can be expressed as an interest towards what's happening in the community as well as through active participation in solving some of the local problems." The Workshop for Civic Initiatives Foundation (WCIF).

Hoping to help address some of the local problems, students in the "Social Responsibility" course, as academic learners, wanted to learn about the needs of the local women—the housewives. When questioning what they could do for the women living in Kayışdağı, they aspired to make a call and reach the women of the local community, declaring, "Here we are!"

The aim was to help housewives living near the university campus contribute to their families' budgets with the products they created.

Objective:

To motivate housewives who are not active in business life to create products so that they may gain self-confidence.

Their slogan was:

If there is nobody, "Here we are!" and "Being 'We' is always better than being 'I' ".

"Are you ready to become one of us? "

2008

The results of the field study showed that the women had no active life; some of them were not working and most of them needed financial support.

Ten housewives were invited to the university. They were informed about the project and their demands were identified.

Their interest areas were determined and yarn and jewelry equipment was provided to them.

Their productions would be exhibited for sale at the university before the New Year.

In December, objects such as woolen socks, necklaces, bracelets, and knitted wraps were ready for sale as New Year presents.

Through word-of-mouth promotion, people at the university were informed of the products that were for sale before the New Year.

Reactions:
At the end of the semester, the participating women said their lives were happier and added that they felt more productive due to their small contributions to the family budget.

They were surprised and happy to have met university students for the first time, who helped them.

One of the housewives, who had lost her husband, said that with the support of the young students she felt herself becoming stronger. Instead of staying at home doing nothing, they started knitting and making jewelry.

In 2016, some of the women wanted to learn English and our students were willing to teach them. The mothers worked hard and were proud of themselves. Classes lasted one semester.

"Here We Are" A Call to the Women of Kayışdağı for Solidarity

The products of the local housewives were exhibited at the University by the students before the New Year to be bought as presents

Meral Aydın, Gizem Bakırtaş, Gökçe Karaçizmeli, Burcu Şimşek, Zeynep Gence, Hande Özçelik, Özra Mavioğlu, Sinan Işın, Uğur Peyman, Melis Toroslu, Ceren Aşkın, Alex Dekesoğlu, Pelin Toksal, Melis Akpeçe, Atalay

40 Social Responsibility Courses as Local and Global Academic Learning

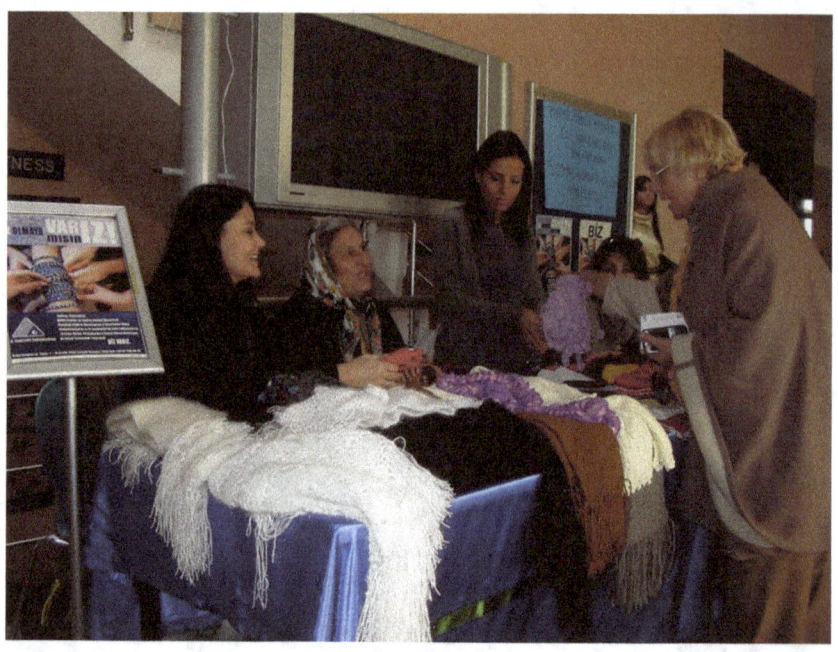

"Good Luck" beads were the favorite presents of the students...

"Social Responsibility Project for Graduation" Course

The academic learning course Social Responsibility Project for Graduation is designed to empower students to become more thoughtful and supportive citizens and to build a culture of solidarity between the students and the local community. Going beyond the conventional role of universities in what we can do for the local community was asked.

To answer the need of the local community, each semester since 2010, students have been divided into two groups—one group visits the residents of the care home near the university campus, and the other group invites the primary school children living in Kayışdağı around the campus to help with their homework.

The project aims for the students to internalize their feeling of responsibility. In the beginning of the semester, the students are assigned to groups according to their choices, and making the choice is not easy for them. They are torn between their prejudiced feelings concerning the groups: between "wiping the tears" or "keeping up with the naughty kids".

How the students should communicate—practicing intercultural communication and empathy—was important. They practice the Communication Accommodation Theory (CAT) and behave accordingly.

At the end of the semester, students hand in the presentations and PowerPoints or videos covering their activities, as well as reflection papers or stories about their observations and feelings.

The students of the Public Relations and Publicity Department completed their Social Responsibility Project for Graduation course, calling it "From 7 to 77 Intergenerational Solidarity".

During the stay-at-home due to COVID-19 our young students continued their social responsibility doing the shopping for the senior relatives or neighbors or teaching their children.

At the Care Home in Kayışdağı

Elderly care has not been an issue or a problem to consider seriously in Turkey until recently. Traditionally, the elderly who, like everyone else in the extended family, contributed to the family in one way or another were cared for. With industrialization, urbanization, and modernization, however, the extended family life started to dissolve. Urban residences were not sufficient for co-residence of the extended family, and "modern" young couples preferring a nuclear family refused to co-reside with the elderly. This brought up the issue of elderly care to be solved by families and society, so nursing care homes for the elderly were sought to solve the problem. Today in the Anatolian regions of the country, elderly nursing homes are either unpopular or non-existent because leaving one's parents in a care home is still considered a disgrace to the family there; in the big cities, however, the shortage of both private and public care home services continues.

A Handful of Love and Respect

There are both private and public care homes near Kayışdağı. The public one was established in 1998 as an institution of the İstanbul Municipality to take care of old people who have no relatives. It is the biggest care home with 10 buildings in a large green park. They all provide health care, food, education, and clothing. In the beginning of the semester, we ask for permission to send our students to visit the residents during the semester, giving the students' names and getting identification cards for them. We are thankful to the management and officers for accepting our students and sending the residents to our university for the mutual organizations we arrange.

Loneliness in a Crowd

Describing their first meeting at the care home, the young students, looking into the eyes of the residents of the care home, who later became their "aunts" and "uncles", felt their longing for love and interest. They realized that "feeling lonely may be bad but feeling lonely in a crowd—among other people— is the worst". The young students thought they would be grief counselors, fellow sufferers, sympathetic ears, or a shoulder to cry on.

For me, the lonely man playing his flute (kaval) best symbolizes the loneliness that the residents of the care home feel, and it is one of the most impressive memories in my mind.

As time went on, our students became the "grandchildren" of the residents, who kept asking them to come back. Seeing the sparkle in the smiling faces, young students started calling them "aunts" and "uncles". They realized the importance of intercultural communication and empathy in their approach to the senior residents. They felt like "they became a family", and they listened to different life stories and looked at their old photos together.

They all felt both joy and sorrow at the same time and love and respect for the personality of the people. They all shared laughter and tears, sang songs, formed a knitting team, had a picnic outside in the garden, tried learning crochet or playing backgammon, enjoyed drinking tea and coffee, and learned their fortune after drinking Turkish coffee. The aunts and uncles read their fortune in the coffee cup and vice versa.

Most of the residents opened their hearts to them. One uncle told one of the young girls, "This is a life university, and we are your teachers," so she wrote down what she learned from each teacher. From one teacher, she learned to be honest; from another, she learned to accept sorrow gracefully and never give up. She also learned about the importance of travel, discussing politics, new songs to sing, and, most importantly, being a human being.

The reflection papers they handed in reveal that most of them felt they have become mature young people. They realized that each individual is a different world—each has a different story and a different piece of advice to give to the young students. Nearly all of the young students put into the words the importance of kindness and respect while approaching the aunts and uncles in the care home. Most of them realized and made it clear that the personality of the individual is what is important.

Some of them said, "When I met them, it was as if I met my grandparents" and questioned human relations.

Concluding Comments by Students

"We built a 'bridge between generations', established a connection with them every week and shared our feelings, thoughts, and, especially, smiles."

"I now know that there is no happiness greater than making other people happy—just holding hands may be enough."

"Every day, I went there with excitement and left with peace in my heart."

"Thank you for assigning us such great responsibility."

"They all left unforgettable traces in our lives."

"It is not difficult to make them happy. Just a sincere hello can brighten their faces."

The experience was humanizing and uplifting for both parties.

Warm hugs, kisses, and the look in their eyes are the unforgettable "thank you" messages one gets at the care home.

If we could get the permission, the pictures would reflect the warm and caring relationships created between "nieces /nephews" and "aunts/uncles" when students started addressing the elderly as "aunt" or "uncle". Senior residents in the care home liked their pictures taken and ask to get their copies; they enjoy seeing their pictures. The pictures of dear Güler Sarı, the "flute (kaval) player uncle", and the "philosopher uncle" will live in our memories. They would love to be in our book.

The poem "aunt" Cahide wrote on loneliness moved us all.

> Flowers don't bloom here
> Birds don't fly gliding/floating
> Stars don't shine
> Days don't pass by
> In life unive it is spring outside
> There are people walking by
> Days pass by like water
> Days don't pass by, don't pass by

A "Thank you" note from a senior resident given to our students:

With your students you made us happy; your shining faces are the mirrors of your souls. May God make you happy...

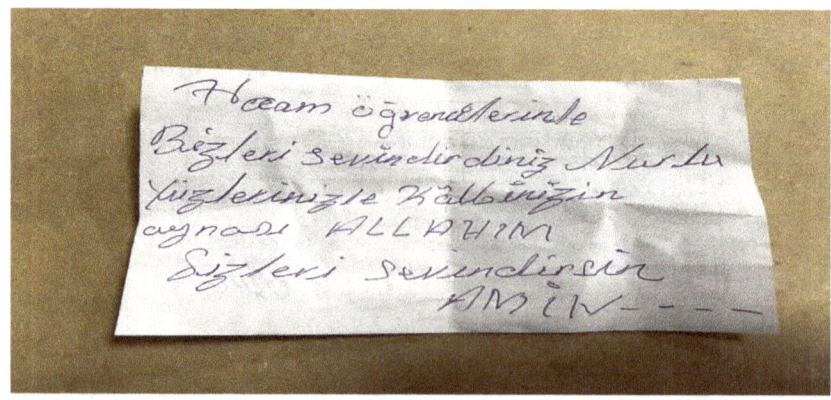

"Social Responsibility Project for Graduation" Course

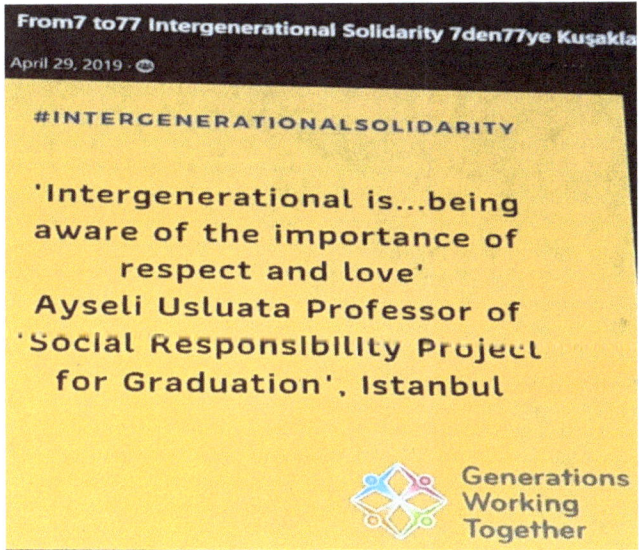

Knitting, singing, celebrating national holidays, outdoor visits, doing make-up/ nail polishing, fortune-telling after drinking Turkish coffee, writing letters, sharing life-stories, playing chess—all these activities were enlightening and enriching,.

Knitting needles and wool were the best presents for the "aunts" at the care home...

New Year presents on the way

"Social Responsibility Project for Graduation" Course

Our musician uncle while waiting for our visit plays his pipe...

Fresh in our memories...

A surprise present European Map of Intergenerational Learning

- Yeditepe University Semester – Intergenerational Project

Newsletter – 25th edition

Yeditepe University Pictures featured in this Newsletter

Yeditepe University students of Public Relations and Publicity Faculty Department visited the Care Home in the vicinity of the University Campus as they do every semester for their Graduation Project. This semester they were assigned to visit the home hosting older women who were confined to bed. Project coordinator – Professor Usluata says her students became like daughters or granddaughters, sons or Grandsons for those who are all bedridden.

Pictures throughout this latest edition of the EMIL newsletter include images of the students listening to residents life stories and reading stories of famous authors; listening to music together while looking out of the window and enjoying the beautiful nature; drawing pictures together to make the hand muscles move and get stronger; as well as enjoying the colourful pictures and having them put up on the walls the care home.

If you have any questions about this project, please contact the coordinator Professor Dr. Ayseli Usluata: ausluata@yahoo.com

"Social Responsibility Project for Graduation" Course

This picture highlights the benefit of art work in improving the wellbeing of older people in care homes. Young students'' initiative brought creativity into the lives of bed-ridden people in care i .

It shows how participation in painting, art work and music and dance, can benefit them, with a powerful and positive effect. Reading books, newspapers can soothe and stimulate at the same time, bringing back memories from the past.

Breaking Down the Walls

Change a Child, the Whole World Changes!

Social Responsibility for Graduation students decided to open the doors of the campus and invite the primary school children living in the neighborhood and their families to the campus to help the schoolchildren with their lessons.

Naming their project "We are breaking down the walls of the campus", they meant "There will be no walls between us; we are your older brothers and sisters." They have been teachers, as well as older brothers and sisters, of the primary school children since 2009.

The literature about children, education, and change exhibits the slogans used by different national or international institutions, organizations or foundations. For the Turkish Education Foundation (TEV), it is "A child changes, Turkey develops"; for Turkish environmentalist foundations (TEGV and TURNEPA), "A child develops, the world changes"; and for UNICEF, "A chance to change the world with children".

As young university students, our students, declaring, "They are our future," took the chance to be the older brothers and sisters of the Kayışdağ primary school children and educate them to change their future and society.

Great Love of Tiny Hearts

The happiness of seeing the sparkle in the smiling faces and of having the cheerful kids jump up to embrace their "older brothers and sisters" during the semester was reflected in the stories of the students at the end of the semester. In the reflection papers covering their experiences, observations, impressions, and evaluations, the different perspective of each individual story was very impressive.

Love Increases When Shared

The children were silent at first, trying to get used to their young teachers, but the warm interest of our young students let them be the older brothers and sisters of the children and gave the classes an enjoyable atmosphere. The children were afraid of making mistakes, but they gained self-confidence. They lacked general culture, so students worked on that.

The families around the campus are immigrants from different cities in Anatolia. The children were 3rd-, 4th- and 5th-grade students who went to school either in the morning or in the afternoon. In the crowded classes at the public primary schools, they could not get enough help or attention both at school and at home. Our students were ready to support them in their lessons, to be their role models, and to socialize with them.

A Chance to Change Local and Global Communities with Children

The amazing teaching program designed by our students according to their fields of interest in 2011 shows that our students used the chance for the best. The course schedule included social studies, mathematics, citizenship and environment, physical education, English, Turkish, drawing, and folk dances. The topics were ideal, and the role models were excellent in changing the children—who will one day change the world—of the local community, Kayışdağı. Knowing their rights and respecting and tolerating the rights of others can help them become individuals. In the classroom, the students asked questions, such as "What is life?" and "What is happiness?" They tried to find answers with examples that children can understand.

They learned about climate, natural disasters, children's rights, different countries, geography, music, painting, and basketball. While learning and practicing the technical part, the kids also learned how to breathe, play as a team, and concentrate on one point. They learned how to hold a pen to draw a line, and at the end, the kids painted "happiness" and "unhappiness".

They shared all their observations with the parents. What made them happy was the sensitivity of the parents to the young student teachers' comments, statements, and suggestions.

Achievements

They did not know English at all, and at the end of the semester, they sang songs to the audience in English.

At the university's cinema hall, they watched animated films for kids.

Visiting the children's museum was an exciting event for the children.

The children wrote poems for their older brothers and sisters/teachers to show their appreciation and love.

The positive feedback from the parents and the school teachers motivated our students and made us all proud of them.

They tried to integrate them into university; we saw that students of other faculties loved them as well. While taking photos, from time to time, even the university personnel wanted to take part in the pictures.

The primary school children learned about different countries and their capitals, climate, natural disasters, the geography of Turkey, and subjects dealing with general culture. They gained interest in the lessons.

They found out one student was very good at math, another had talent in learning and speaking English, one boy had an extraordinary ability in drawing, and a girl was very successful in playing basketball.

What Our Senior Students as Teachers Learned

"Teaching is difficult but at the same time rewarding. Letting kids express themselves helps them to gain self-confidence. Adding fun makes learning enjoyable and unforgettable. Assigning homework makes children responsible."

"What we have achieved was useful for the kids, but it was more valuable and useful for us."

"As a senior student until now, I have never thought about how heavy a burden teaching is and how sacred it is to be a teacher."

Our students learned that every child has a different personality and a different way of understanding.

They found out that teaching is a job that needs a lot of patience and interest. With the realization of the importance of responsibility, their responsibility consciousness developed. They experienced the pleasure of being helpful and being able to reach out to the children.

Reactions

"We are happy to have given a hand to our younger brothers and sisters in Kayışdağı and contributed to their education and development."

"Sharing knowledge is delightful."

"It was not easy to teach them English, so we used songs and helped them to like English."

"We found out one of them was good at math, another had a talent in speaking English, one boy had an extraordinary ability in drawing, and a girl was very successful in playing basketball."

"We became a lovely family, sometimes friends, and then teachers. We sang songs."

"A wonderful semester altogether with smiling faces, shining eyes, warm laughter, and, sometimes, tears for no reason. Pure, innocent feelings, asking before the lesson, 'Teacher, what will we learn today?'"

"We will never forget the eyes looking at the future with hope and sincere love."

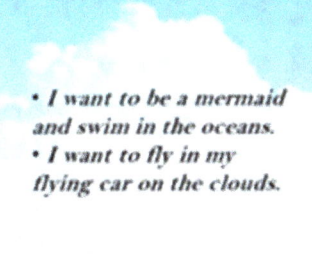

- *I want to be a mermaid and swim in the oceans.*
- *I want to fly in my flying car on the clouds.*

54 Social Responsibility Courses as Local and Global Academic Learning

56 Social Responsibility Courses as Local and Global Academic Learning

A visit to the Children's Museum

"Social Responsibility Project for Graduation" Course

Children to Change the Society/Nation

Ege and Efe Yalçın are brothers who have regularly attended the courses of our project. Their mother accompanied them to the campus, where they took the shuttle bus to the faculty building, and waited for her sons with the other mothers until the class finished and then accompanied them back home. Now, they are successful high school students. Their English skills are better than those of other students and they proudly declare that their "elder brothers and sisters" at Yeditepe University were their English teachers. The brothers both play musical instruments in their spare time. They are going forward.

58 Social Responsibility Courses as Local and Global Academic Learning

Yeditepe University 2015 Ege is reading a poem for the "23rd April Children's Holiday" at our Global Classroom to the American students.
   Two brothers at the dinner party, Yeditepe University
   Ege–High school graduate and Efe–highschool student 2020

Members of the İldeş family, Elif, Ömer, Sabri, and Irem—two sisters and two brothers—are former participants of our project. They are now working hard to achieve their goal of attending university to study natural sciences and the ecosystem. Our students are using this chance to educate children who will change the whole world.

"Social Responsibility Project for Graduation" Course

Elif, Ömer, Merve and Sabri: İldeş sisters and brothers

A Letter from the Father of 4 Children

Dear, very precious teaching angel,

Hope you are healthy. I am Adil Ömer, Merve İrem and Muhammed Sabri's father, Vasıf İldeş. Do you remember me? Precious Teacher, you are very kind. In this time when nobody greets each other, you are interested in trying to educate our children. As an educator, you surprise us and make us happy. We had been living next door to the university wondering what was behind the walls but couldn't enter. You opened the doors for us. We entered, walked around, and saw inside because of you, and we are very happy.

Hello Life!

Young students who need special attention

Joining the "Hello Life" project made our senior student Şevval Giril's dream come true. Her autistic older brother was in the "Hello Life Education Workshop" ("Hayata Merhaba Project" Yunus Emre). This workshop, through the initiative of Ms. Emine Koçak, was founded to help young students who need special attention. It aims to prepare them for life by teaching them how to produce objects for sale, such as cloth bags and ornaments, and by helping them find employment. For years, Şevval's dream was for her friends to meet her older brother. Together with our senior students, we talked to Ms. Koçak and a group of our students decided to regularly visit the workshop as part of our course project. This made Şevval happy. After the group visit, the smiling faces of our students made us all happy.

Football matches on the campus and activities in the conference hall brought together the students, friends of "Hello Life" and visitors of different generations, uniting them.

Reflection

Before meeting our friends in the workshop, we were unsure whether we would be able to communicate well with them and were questioning ourselves. However, we were successful in doing so because the delightful young people enlightened us. The most meaningful contribution was to be able to look at the world through their eyes. When I first met them, they approached me as if I were their teacher and they felt I could enlighten them. When they laughed, the beauty of their hearts was reflected on their faces. I learned a lot from them. The smiles on their faces and the purity of their hearts connected us. We were successful.

Football matches on the campus and the activities in the in the conference hall brought the students, the friends of "Hello Life" and the visitors of different generations altogether, uniting them.

At the Workshop of "Hello Life"

Our students visited their friends at the workshop to see their products and help them.
Happy sister!

On the Yeditepe Campus: Football match with the Yeditepe students and the joy of being the winner

62 Social Responsibility Courses as Local and Global Academic Learning

"Hello Life!" friends loved the University campus.

"Social Responsibility Project for Graduation" Course

At the Conference Hall
Burcu Haznedaroğlu introduces the new friends...

64 Social Responsibility Courses as Local and Global Academic Learning

Joint Intergenerational Activities

Activities such as concerts and folklore performances organized by the students brought two or four generations together and united them at the university; they danced, sang songs, watched themselves in videos and had dinner. Additional activities included a boat trip along the Bosphorus as well as other social events organized by our students. The university provided transportation.

One of the district mayors in Istanbul provided a boat for our students so that they could take a group of care home residents for a boat trip along the Bosphorus.

Primary school children prepared folk dance accompanying the music. (Their older sister teachers arranged the show) Hülya Selen

European Map of Intergenerational Learning

Newsletter – 21st edition

INTERGENERATIONAL Mothers' Day Celebration

To celebrate Mothers' Day in Istanbul, Turkey a group of students from Yeditepe University invited residents of a nearby elderly home and primary school kids living in the same district to the University. These university students had been visiting the residents of the care home during the semester, in groups of 3 or 4, listening to their life stories, taking photos, playing cards with the elderly as well as helping the kids in the district with their homework and teaching them English. After snacks and social gathering the grandmothers and grandchildren were ushered to the conference hall where they listened to the kids singing songs and reciting poems and watched themselves in the videos the University students had made with the photos they had taken. Then each kid presented a red carnation to a grandmother and they all danced.

At the end of each semester students invite both the residents of the care home and the kids of Kayışdağı to share with them the power-point presentations they have create with the pictures they have taken during their visits. We all revive the memories of solidarity.

The University Folklor Club students with their dances fascinated the residents of the care home who were invited to dinner party at the dining hall of the university.

Social Responsibility Projects During the Lockdown 2020

During the pandemic lockdown period for their academic learning course students of Social Responsibility Project for Graduation were very creative in choosing their individual projects. In their engagement with the community at the end of the semester each of them came up with power-point presentations and stories revealing their giving and receiving. Their pictures and writings reflected their improved competencies, such as critical thinking, self-confidence, teamwork, leadership, communication skills and problem solving, but the most important gain for them all was "sharing love" with all living creatures and nature.

A Collection from the Project Stories and Comments of Students

Pelin Başak

In today's world there are so many problems that need to be dealt with. As young individuals we need to know our responsibilities towards our society. One of the ways of making young people take responsibility about the issues in their environments is integrating a social responsibility course into higher education. In this paper, I will talk about the importance of higher education and social responsibility course and my experiences.

I do believe the civic education should be integrated more into higher learning since it is important for students to have further information addressing problems in the world. The organization called Project Pericles is committed to help students to become more engaged and responsible citizens. The founder, Eugene M. Lang, explains the importance of this project by stating that the future of a country as a just, compassionate democracy depends on young people and their understanding and their awareness of their society and its needs. "As a regular part of their educational missions, colleges and universities should provide students with a sense of social and civic responsibility—that as advocates of their thoughtful judgments, they can make a difference" (Liss and Liazos, 2010).

I also think it is very important to encourage the students to make a difference in the society they are part of. Empowering students to become more thoughtful and effective citizens will increase their understandings of being socially responsible. "Integrating perspectives that varied by discipline, class, gender, race, ethnicity, and political persuasion helped students understand and respect multiple points of view on issues of social concern, a crucial ability for citizens in a democratic society" (Liss and Liazos, 2010). Having such education increases the empathy since one can see the issues from multiple perspectives. It also inspires students to become more active in their communities.

Moreover, Dr. Rajesh Tandon, UNESCO Chair in Community-Based Research and Social Responsibility in Higher Education, explains that social responsibility has given them a new meaning to work on making higher education relevant to our societies. Since the mission of higher education is to serve society, public purpose therefore it should be integrated with social responsibility.

I would like to talk about my project and my experiences. As my project I chose to give English lessons to middle grade and high school students. According to the article "Faculty in the social sciences also found that projects that served a real purpose in the community deepened student enthusiasm and learning" (Liss and Liazos, 2010). The project I did, definitely cultivated a deeper sense of commitment and engagement to what I was doing.

While choosing my project I paid more attention to how I can use my voice to connect with my students, showing them my absolute sincerity.

My method of helping my students has been from in front of our computers. I was frustrated and disappointed about not seeing them in person and helping them in a more sincere environment. In one part of the article, anthropologist Kim Jones of Elon University explains this by saying "In the real world, things don't always happen as you might expect, and it is important to process these difficulties collectively as an important part of experiential learning. It is important for students not to get frustrated and disappointed when structural barriers prevent them from being able to do everything they wish they could do for the community" (Liss and Liazos, 2010). Even though Covid-19 made things a lot harder, with patience and perseverance I was able to overcome it.

In conclusion, social responsibility is an important matter and its integration to the higher education benefits both society and the young individuals. This class, made me realize the impacts I can make in society. Furthermore, seeing my friends sharing what they have done on Facebook made me so proud and it deepened my interest into this class.

"Be the change that you want to see in the world"
Ghandi
Reference
Liss, J., Liazos, A. (2010). Incorporating Education for Civic and Social Responsibility. *Change Magazine*, 45–50

"Social Responsibility Project for Graduation" Course

What Is My Project?

My project was to teach English to middle grade and high school students. For this reason I contacted with three students from Gebze and both taught them new things and helped in their homeworks.

İrem Ceylan

The concept of social responsibility has an increasing importance today. Social responsibility constitutes the basis of service to society. Universities aim to train students as individuals who are sensitive to the society with the courses they have created together with their educational programs. They enable students to serve the society with the projects they implement. We can define the concept of social responsibility as the individuals' regulation of their behavior by considering social consequences. The main goal of social responsibility approach is to provide social benefit and to make a difference in the general or part of the society.

Education plays an important role in improving the life quality of both individuals and all humanity. Education systems that aim to provide students with only theoretical knowledge cannot function adequately in terms of increasing the quality of life. In order for education to increase the quality of life, it should also gain awareness of social responsibility, such as taking into account the perspectives of others and contributing to communities. Sheri Berman stated: "Social responsibility does not happen automatically; it requires desire, attention and time." Based on this idea, we can say that students cannot be expected to gain awareness of social responsibility on their own. A student who experiences social responsibility will have a lifelong gain. They do this by taking an active role in social responsibility activities, contributing to the solution of problems, and acquiring these various skills. Providing social responsibility education at universities has another importance. It has the power to give young people the ability to act in the face of events with a sense of self-confidence.

According to the results of Jerry Bachman's survey of 17,000 high school students every year, in the surveys conducted after 1978, approximately 45 % of the students stated that "I feel there is little I can do to change the world" (Berman, 1990). According to the results of this survey, half of the students feel powerless. . Social responsibility courses given at universities give students a sense of self-confidence. It allows them to take an active part in finding solutions to problems after graduation and to look to the future with more hope. As a conclusion it is very important for universities to include course programs in the field of social responsibility so that the individuals they are educating are sensitive to the society and the world. While contributing to students, universities also reveal their own social responsibility approaches. Social responsibility courses should improve students' ability to produce solutions for results. Teaching social responsibility courses at universities has the potential to help students acquire the necessary knowledge, skills, values, and motivation to take action in their communities as thoughtful, engaged, and socially responsible citizens.

References

Berman, S. (1990) Educating For Social Responsibility. Service Learning, General. Paper 11, 75–80

Liss, J.R., & Liazos, A. (2010). Incorporating Education for Civic and Social Responsibility into the Undergraduate Curriculum. Change: The Magazine of Higher Learning, 42, 45 – 50.

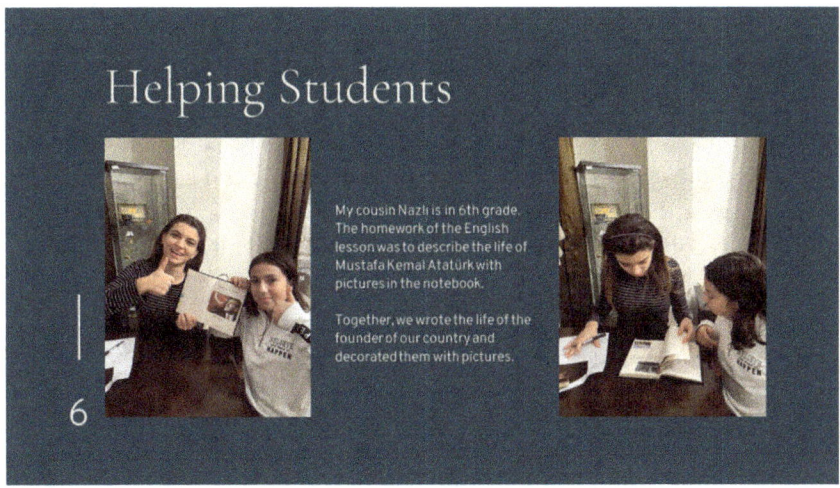

Selin Budak

As a student of the Social Responsibility course at our university I wanted to be able to see and understand our social responsibilities from different angles, and the article of Liss & Liazos (2010) provided me the opportunity to gain academic knowledge about social responsibilities and to take action in solving these problems and improving conditions in our society. While fulfilling my social responsibilities, I sometimes took action on supplying food to people in need. Sometimes I gave food to the stray animals that were

76 Social Responsibility Courses as Local and Global Academic Learning

always around me, and met their shelter and health needs. One of the most important information I learned while performing my Social Responsibility activities is that an individual should be trained on this subject at a younger age. In every step I carried out my project, I tried to teach the awareness of social responsibility to the young children around me, and seeing that I really achieved success as a result of these efforts was one of the steps that made me the happiest and informed me about the necessity of social responsibility. Because of all these experiences, I see social responsibility as an activity of responsibility that an individual should carry out for his/her family, environment, society and values, therefore, I think that the social responsibility lesson that we have seen in our faculty is very necessary. At the same time, I learned that as people help, they find themselves in a completely different world of emotions when they share someone's smile or the joy of a tiny animal. I am very happy that I came to this point by taking the social responsibility lesson and chose this lesson.

As stated in the video prepared by the Presidency of UNESCO, social responsibility projects are one of the most important assets that inspire, renew and make people happy. I think that teaching social responsibility as a course and spreading it in universities will make great contributions not only to countries but also to world societies globally.

"Social Responsibility Project for Graduation" Course

Yaşar Mert Bilgin

I took many courses during my university life, these courses improved me in learning to analyse and to think rationally, but the course that affected and developed me the most was my social responsibility course. It was one of the courses I enjoyed the most throughout my university life because, in the courses I have taken up to now, what I learned were about improving the reputation of institutions and companies, product promotions and so on. We were dealing with these issues. However, there are more important issues for me than these. Helping others. solidarity and people's tolerance towards each other are more important issues for me. The perception of "everything is money" created by the capitalist system and selfishness of people can be overcome by social responsibility projects and socialization of people with each other. Unfortunately, these people are isolated due to the desire of people thinking about themselves and earning money. They are not happy, but if they go out and help a person in need, they will enjoy the feeling so much that their desire to earn money will become secondary. When the awareness of social responsibility develops, even class differences can disappear.

I would like to talk about my feelings while doing my social responsibility projects.

Visiting children living in orphanages in order to make them feel that they are not alone and that there is a group that cares about them was my first social responsibility project, but instead of visiting not to endanger the health of the children due to the pandemic I sent them gifts Looking at their photos, I was very happy to see the expressions on their faces. I lived one of the happiest moments in my life. The purpose for doing this project was to make it clear that I was with them.

My other project was about the doctors at the time of the pandemic. I wanted to show our gratitude to the healthcare professionals who sacrificed their lives for our lives. Our healthcare workers could not eat because the cafeterias in the hospital were closed due to the pandemic. We sent meals and desserts from our homes to ease their long working conditions. I wanted to let them know that we are with them.

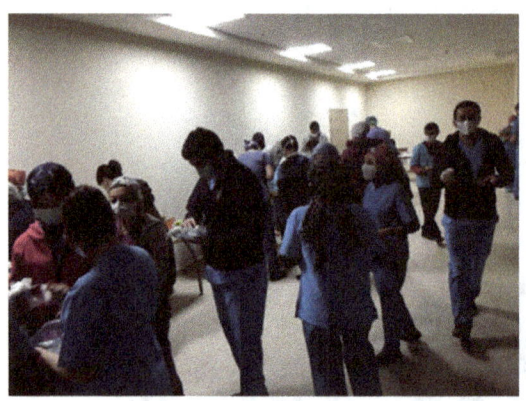

Enes Malik Öztürk

This course was very different from the courses of traditional education we are used to. This "difference" that I mentioned is a difference in a positive sense because this course does not progress by reading theoretical things at the desk like other courses, in this course we do something real, and these things are social responsibility projects.

"Social Responsibility Project for Graduation" Course

We spent a long emotionless time at the university with courses such as marketing and brand images. Even if it covered simple tasks due to the pandemic, doing social responsibility projects reminded me of our humanitarian side. For this course our activities were limited due to the pandemic, but I believe that university students, with the experience of academics, recognize great potential for social responsibility projects. Such activities should be expanded.

Many young people now focus solely on career or academic success. Some of them spend their time having fun irresponsibly. However, we do not sufficiently protect people and living things in need of attention and help which is a situation that alienates the society within itself. Although alienation or loneliness in society seems to be an individual thing, it is actually a contagious problem at least as much as "covid". Solving this problem can be prevented by not ignoring the problems of the individuals who make up the society. I am also a student with a minor in sociology. Social responsibility projects enable individuals to adapt to changes in society more easily, and provide strengthened social ties by solving social and individual problems. These are very important factors because negative actions such as crime rates, suicidal acts, and depression are somewhat inversely proportional to the strength of social ties.

80 Social Responsibility Courses as Local and Global Academic Learning

Why I chose to feed street animals visiting older people or giving lessons to young students, would be risky because of pandemic. In Turkey streets are full of cats and dogs.

Few months ago a cat gave birth in the empty field across the place where I work. When I noticed that they are hungry, I decided to feed them.

Oğuzhan Ceyhan
Maybe our social responsibility projects have been limited due to the pandemic, but we have overcome these difficulties in line with the information provided by our instructor. The important thing was to start. I helped people who participated in my projects to spread these activities around. For the most part, people, especially young people in our age, are very focused on success, more interested in things that pay off. They work like robots for this, but while doing this, we forget or do not see the lonely people and animals that are hungry around us. In the past, this situation was not serious compared to now. Especially in a digitalized world, we forgot each other. People's phones have become more valuable than those around them. We remember these solidarities when something bad happens to us. In fact, this is wrong and unpleasant, we should keep cooperation and interaction at the highest level even when life continues in its normal flow. Our award needs to be high.

- The factor that influenced me in choosing this project was that I wanted to be around stray animals.

- While doing this project, we managed to reach all the animals in our streets with the contribution of small children in our neighborhood.

- We tried to take care of each street animal. Some of them were checked through veterinarians we knew.

- As another project, we did additional history lessons with Pırıl. We tried to close the gap as much as possible.

- Our lessons, which we organized 3 times so far, have been productive. It was a nice feeling to be able to add something to the little ones.

Cansu Kuşcu

Social responsibility projects are effective projects that enable societies to be in solidarity and reveal unseen problems. It is especially important for us students to produce or support projects on issues that will raise awareness. We are extremely proud that Yeditepe University focuses on this issue and is taught as a course for us students. I hope it catches the same awareness in all universities soon. Thanks to this lesson, we realized that there are people other than ourselves, we are not alone in this world. The elderly, children and animals around us are part of the world we live in and everyone should be aware of this. This course gave me light to create a better world.

Social responsibility projects not only support the personal development of the individual, but also contribute to their educational life and academic performance. For this reason, from kindergarten to university, children should take theoretical and practical lessons in the field of social responsibility as much as a mathematics course. For this reason, they can both develop their own motor skills while having the opportunity to get to know the society they live in more closely. Students who implement their own social responsibility projects in their academic life will be able to develop many skills such as organization, communication, effective presentation, public speaking, respect for awareness, self-confidence, etc.

82 Social Responsibility Courses as Local and Global Academic Learning

Naz Tandoğan
I think everyone should have respect and contribution to the environment where they live and those living around them. It is necessary to understand this as well as to have a lesson that shows how to do it. Because sometimes even people know what they want to do but don't know how to do it and where to start. I think this lesson will help with such problems and remove obstacles. And sometimes, they cannot find the strength to do certain things in theirself. So I believe this course is a move to action. In addition to being a move to action, I also think there is a sustainable part. As people start to contribute to their environment, they both touch and encourage other people's lives.

I also think that this course is also teaching us how to overcome and end the problems around us, rather than help and contribution. So I strongly advocate that this course should be taught worldwide. Even though it sounds like a small thing, I believe it will produce very effective improvements.

Aleyna Sayın

Universities have an important place in the development of social responsibility awareness. The theoretical courses given at the university improve the mission of the students, but different from these theoretical courses "Social Responsibility Course" develops the vision of the students. Dr. Rajesh Tandon The UNESCO –Co-Chair in Community- Based Research and Socially Responsible Higher Education, in 5 words describes social Responsibility education as "stimulating, satisfying, refreshing, challenging and inspiring".

Helping people and animals in need in different parts of society, meeting their needs, in short, contributing to society gives students great awareness. Students who gain this awareness begin to think "community" instead of thinking "I" oriented. Thus, it helps students to develop community awareness and also contributes to the formation of character. In the article "Incorporating Education for Social Responsibility into the Undergraduate Curriculum", Eugene M. Lang, founder of Project Pericles says; "Our country's future as a just, compassionate democracy depends on young people—their understanding and civic responsiveness to society's needs and issues of social change. As a regular part of their educational missions, colleges and universities should provide students with a sense of social and civic responsibility as advocates of their thoughtful judgments, and they can make a difference." With the Social Responsibility Course, students learn not to stand by against social events and social needs. They not only learns this consciousness theoretically, but also implement it in practice. It provides the training of individuals who produce solutions and think solution-oriented. In a way, when social responsibility is given, knowledge becomes an experience. With the Social Responsibility Course, students provide more permanent learning by experience. They reconcile the knowledge they learn with the outside world.

With the Social Responsibility Course, students wash down their assumptions and realize their prejudices and get rid of these prejudices. Young individuals who are sensitive to society are raised. In addition, it develops the communication skills of students. Their ability to empathize increases. From this point of view, the perception of "desensitization" of young individuals towards society is also eliminated. Because they take an active role in society. It allows students to be more thoughtful and effective citizens. Helping people, animals in need and doing so without waiting for reciprocity improves students' awareness of social responsibility, and the development of this consciousness contributes greatly to individuals in their future life. Students learn to look at social problems from a broader perspective and gain new perspectives.

With my Social Responsibility Project, I helped children and touched their lives. During the pandemic, their school life had entered a very difficult period and they had difficulty adapting to this process. By helping them with their homework, preparing for the exams together, I lightened the burden on their shoulders. When my students were successful, I was proud of them. The Social Responsibility Course was a good opportunity for me and for them.

I've won a lot of awareness by taking a Social Responsibility Course. Instead of waiting or expecting good events to happen on behalf of the community, I took action. I realized that I could contribute a little bit to the benefit of society, and most importantly, I saw these little contributions grow like a snowball. My friends and I have carried out very successful Social Responsibility Projects and we have seen how beautiful and effective activities can emerge when everyone steps up. The Social Responsibility Course has been an important lesson that sheds light on our future.

"Social Responsibility Project for Graduation" Course

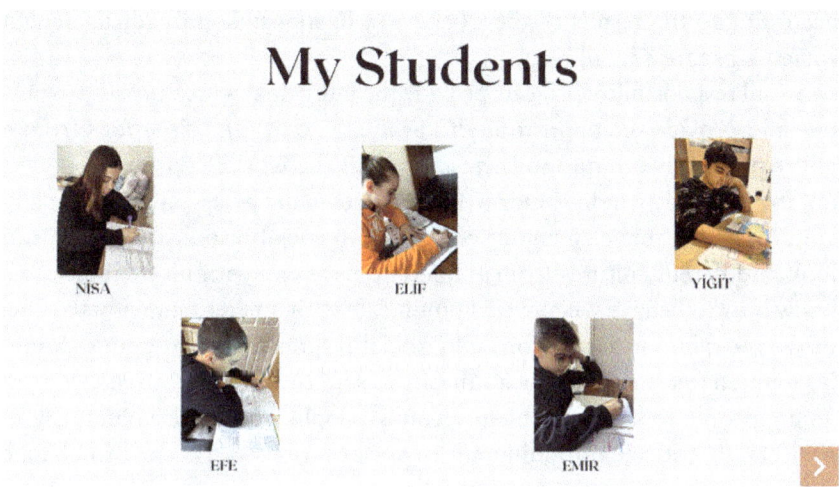

Aysun Yakar

Social Responsibility and Education

The concept of social responsibility is the actions and formations that take place as a result of considering the interests of the society as well as the individual's own interests. In this respect, social responsibility is important for the sustainability of society. Creating solutions on behalf of society is the main goal of individuals working in this direction. Social responsibility in education is an increasingly important concept.

Education is a phenomenon that changes and affects human life in all aspects. We need the guidance of education to make a difference in our lives. Recently, new courses have been added to academic programs aimed to add socially responsible individuals to the society. Although the success of these courses varies according to some criteria, positive feedback is received from the students. Courses integrated with social responsibility projects inspire students to make a difference while integrating them into society. Social responsibility will continue to be the most necessary phenomenon of our present and future. Our main priority should be to bring socially responsible individuals to society in this field. Social responsibility teaches individuals to be responsible for the problems they encounter and enables them to act according to the results of their behavior. Responsible individuals benefit society's progress in all respects.

Social responsibility projects provide the individual with a broad perspective and provide the opportunity to evaluate events and situations from a wider perspective. It allows them to look at the world from many angles, not from a single window. Our world requires many perspectives with many cultural and ethnic elements it covers. With social responsibility, we can look at different cultures from a different place and without prejudice. We know how to behave when we communicate with different individuals. One of the most important reasons why social responsibility programs should be adapted to academic education can be said to increase the sensitivity of young people to social problems. Young people who work voluntarily in projects do not remain indifferent to social problems, they try to change the society they live in positively. They strive to change social conditions and economic inequalities and make a difference in this area. It is aimed to be beneficial to the society. It is aimed to transform the society in a good way without considering a personal interest.

Keeping the environment clean for the future generations is our social responsibility duty.

Funda Şelik
Higher Education and Social Responsibility Course
Everything is interconnected in life. Especially for people who are in contact with each other. Our ideas come from thousands of sharings. Understanding people is a responsibility for people who cannot live alone.

What we call social responsibility is, in fact, the duty everyone in the society has to fulfill. Old, young, rich, poor etc. our lives are all linked by invisible strings. That's why we should take care of people in our lives as much as we need to take care of our own lives.

Social responsibility is not just about that. Social responsibility is to thank. We show our gratitude to our society, which has had an impact on our past and future.

The social responsibility course, which is an interactive course, gives students different experiences and opens up new horizons thanks to these projects.

For example, although some people are familiar with the concept of helping each other during the growth phase, they have not done much about it, or perhaps haven't found the opportunity. Thanks to this course, many students learn by experiencing the limits of social benefit. Even a single person has a lot of things to share with others. All that is required is to believe in the importance of sharing.

Social responsibility teaches students not to be selfish, but also teaches them to break prejudices. When it is understood that society needs the individual, the process of accepting the society as a whole begins. When a responsible student looks at society, he/she can no longer see uniforms, colors, flags. He sees people who need help.

A higher education student who promises hope has an important place in society. Social responsibility course is necessary for students to gain sensitivity, and taking this course is a big step we have taken for the benefit of society.

Course, students wash down their assumptions and realize their prejudices and get rid of these prejudices. Young individuals who are sensitive to society are raised. In addition, it develops the communication skills of students. Their ability to empathize increases. From this point of view, the perception of "desensitization" of young individuals towards society is also eliminated. Because they take an active role in society. It allows students to be more thoughtful and effective citizens. Helping people, animals in need and doing so without waiting for reciprocity improves students' awareness of social responsibility, and the development of this consciousness contributes greatly to individuals in their future life. Students learn to look at social problems from a broader perspective and gain new perspectives.

With my Social Responsibility Project, I helped children and touched their lives. During the pandemic, their school life had entered a very difficult period and they had difficulty adapting to this process. By helping them with their homework, preparing for the exams together, I lightened the burden on their shoulders. When my students were successful, I was proud of them. The Social Responsibility Course was a good opportunity for me and for them.

What the Students' Reflection Papers Reveal

The students of Public Relations and Publicity who have taken global classroom and social responsibility project courses at Yeditepe University are graduating with self-awareness and new perspectives they have gained through their experiences. These two academic learning courses that connected them with both the local community and the global society have raised their self-awareness. Being both the objects and subjects in the projects they developed, they had the chance to see the world and their country, as well as themselves personally, from the inside out and from the outside in This gave them the opportunity to re-evaluate themselves and their culture. After communicating with students of different countries and cultures, they realized that their personal and cultural stereotypes and prejudices did not fit the reality they were facing, and they began to question the "pictures" in their heads. While exploring other cultures, the students discovered that they themselves were being stereotyped by others as well. Recognizing that being stereotyped is otherization in a way, they tried to see themselves through the eyes of others, and their personal experiences enabled them to erase the pictures in their minds. The same is true for the local community and the society they are part of. This is self-awareness.

The young graduates declared that for a peaceful world to exist, it is our social responsibility to unite, remove barriers, ignore stereotypes, stop marginalizing, and gain self-awareness. They realized that seeing themselves through the eyes of other living beings is important for world peace and is therefore the social responsibility of every individual.

The students complained about and rejected the communication between countries that was provided only through the media; however, since communication has become easier with the development of technology, it is now more accessible to promote our culture and communicate outside of what is shown in the media. Therefore, it should be everyone's responsibility to communicate for the sake of world peace and a better future. The students began to consider how intercultural communication can change stereotypes, i.e. the "pictures" in our minds.

Academic learning presents innovation in higher-education curricula, providing the students the opportunity to experience, learn, and apply various methods of contributing to the society they live in and raising awareness among students on respect and kindness by sharing knowledge and different perspectives.

The reflection papers revealed that the students who created and achieved projects gained self-confidence, new perspectives, and more inquisitive minds, and learned that stereotypes are not a reflection of reality. They became aware of social inequalities, othering, and their prejudices. They learned to overcome their prejudices concerning different cultures, ages, disabilities, and other instances of othering. They showed their appreciation of nature and opened their hearts to other living beings. They questioned the use of "my" instead of "our."

As active young global citizens, students concerned about the future of the "global village" came to the conclusion that building solidarity throughout the world, as well as in their own country and local community, is a must. Among the elements to living together in peace, they suggested love, kindness, equality, justice, dialogue, and mutual understanding. In order to ensure this mutual understanding, self-awareness, respect for each other and for the environment, trust, and intercultural communication skills need to be developed in the academic courses of universities. "Intercultural communication and social responsibility as academic courses should be the most essential requirement for world peace".

> *The teacher is of course an artist, but being an artist does not mean that he or she can make the profile, can shape the students.*
> *What the educator does in teaching is to make it possible for the students to become themselves.*
>
> Paulo Freire

www.ingramcontent.com/pod-product-compliance
Lightning Source LLC
Chambersburg PA
CBHW071832230426
43672CB00013B/2827